Wild and Woolly
ANGORA RABBITS

Marigold Brooks

PowerKiDS press™

New York

Published in 2018 by The Rosen Publishing Group, Inc.
29 East 21st Street, New York, NY 10010

First Edition

Editor: Theresa Morlock
Book Design: Rachel Rising

Photo Credits: Cover, pp. 1, 7 (English Angora), 10 Eric Isselee/Shutterstock.com; Cover (background) Swetlana Wall/Shutterstock.com; Cover. pp.1–24 iStockphoto.com/csdesigns; p. 5 goja1/Shutterstock.com; p. 7 (giant Angora) Maria Dryfhout/Shutterstock.com; p. 7 (satin Angora) https://commons.wikimedia.org/wiki/File:Satinangora.jpg; p. 7 (French Angora) https://commons.wikimedia.org/wiki/File:FrenchAngora.jpg; p. 9 Teresa Levite/Shutterstock.com; p. 11 iStockphoto.com/JuFagundes; p. 12 Oleksandr Lysenko/Shutterstock.com; p. 13 Doug Martin/Science Source/Getty Images; p 14. Mr. SUTTIPON YAKHAM/Shutterstock.com; p 15. HolySource/Shutterstock.com; p. 16 Medvedev Andrey/Shutterstock.com; p. 17 Elena Zakh/Shutterstock.com; p. 18 279photo Studio/Shutterstock.com; p. 19 Grigorita Ko/Shutterstock.com; p. 21 Richard A. Cooke/Corbis Documentary/Getty Images; p. 22 Fiona Ayerst/Shutterstock.com.

Cataloging-in-Publication Data

Names: Brooks, Marigold.
Title: Angora rabbits / Marigold Brooks.
Description: New York : PowerKids Press, 2018. | Series: Wild and woolly | Includes index.
Identifiers: ISBN 9781538325957 (pbk.) | ISBN 9781538325254 (library bound) | ISBN 9781538325964 (6 pack)
Subjects: LCSH: Angora rabbits–Juvenile literature. | Rabbit breeds–Juvenile literature.
Classification: LCC SF455.A5 B76 2018 | DDC 636.932'2–dc23

Manufactured in the United States of America

CPSIA Compliance Information: Batch #BW18PK: For Further Information contact Rosen Publishing, New York, New York at 1-800-237-9932

CONTENTS

Funny Bunnies

If you ever see an Angora rabbit, you might mistake it for a stuffed animal! With their superfluffy fur, **tufty** ears, and round bodies, Angora rabbits are almost too cute to be real.

For hundreds of years, Angora rabbits have been kept as pets and livestock. These animals are gentle and quiet by nature and are somewhat easy to keep. Farmers keep Angora rabbits to **harvest** their wool. Angora wool is valued for its softness and lightness.

Fuzzy Features

China has the highest production of Angora wool.

Angora rabbits come from Turkey. The name "Angora" is believed to have been taken from the original name of Ankara, which is the capital of Turkey.

5

Beautiful Breeds

The American Rabbit Breeders Association (ARBA) is a group that creates standards for rabbit owners in the United States. ARBA recognizes four main breeds, or kinds, of Angora rabbits: English, French, satin, and giant Angoras.

One of the ways you can tell Angora breeds apart is by size. English Angoras are the smallest. They weigh about 7 pounds (3.2 kg). Giant Angoras are the biggest of the breeds. They weigh about 10 pounds (4.5 kg).

Which breed of Angora rabbit do you like best?

Fuzzy Features

Every five years, ARBA publishes a guide called the *Standard of Perfection*. This guide provides details about each rabbit breed.

English Angora

giant Angora

French Angora

satin Angora

7

Fancy Furnishings

Certain parts of an Angora's fur have special names. The fur on an Angora's ears is called fringe. The hair on an Angora's forehead or over its eyes is called bangs. Fur such as fringe and bangs is called furnishings.

Angoras have **layered** fur. A layer of longer, **coarser** fur is called guard hair. The guard hair covers the rabbit's soft undercoat. Rabbit wools have different **textures** depending on the amount of each type of fur.

Fuzzy Features

Rabbits are classified, or sorted into different breeds and groups, based on their features.

English Angoras are the only Angora breed with furnishings on their faces.

9

Cool Colors

Angora rabbits come in many different colors, including black, white, chocolate, blue, lilac, and shades in between. Rabbits that are called "blue" or "lilac" are shades of gray, rather than bright blue or purple. Angora rabbits may have blue, red, or brown eyes.

"Broken" rabbits have fur that's mostly white with spots of brown or black. "Pointed" rabbits have colors on their nose, ears, feet, and tail that differ from the main body color.

10

White rabbits with red eyes are called "ruby-eyed whites" or REWs.

11

Caring for Angoras

A place where **domesticated** rabbits are kept is called a rabbitry. Rabbits like to **burrow**, so it's important not to keep them anywhere with a dirt floor. In most rabbitries, Angoras are kept in wire cages. Rabbits are happiest when they don't have to share their cage with others.

To keep a rabbit healthy, it must be kept clean. Rabbit owners don't put too much bedding inside a rabbit's cage. That could cause their fur to become matted and dirty.

cage ⟶

Rabbits are nervous animals. It's important to be very gentle when touching or holding a rabbit.

13

What do Angora rabbits eat? Pet stores sell rabbit food in the form of pellets, or small pieces. Rabbit pellets are usually made of alfalfa, oats, and other vegetables and grains. Rabbits can also be fed carrots or fresh grass as small treats.

Rabbit owners need to make sure rabbits can reach fresh water and food pellets whenever they want. Owners can also put hay outside a rabbit's cage for it to snack on.

rabbit pellets

There are certain plants rabbits shouldn't eat, such as clover. Before giving a rabbit any nonpellet food, owners must check that it's safe for rabbits to eat.

Angora Life Cycle

Female rabbits are called does. Male rabbits are called bucks. Baby rabbits are called kits or kittens.

Rabbits have babies very quickly. A mother Angora rabbit is **pregnant** for about a month before she has her kits. Angoras have **litters** of up to 15 kits at once!

Angora rabbit kits are very small and weak. Owners make sure a rabbit and her kits are in a safe place where predators, such as foxes, cats, or dogs, can't reach them.

Kits should be kept with their mothers for at least the first eight weeks of their lives.

Grooming and Harvesting

Grooming is the process of cleaning an animal's coat or fur. Angoras need to be groomed regularly even if owners don't plan to sell their wool. Grooming tools include wire brushes, combs, scissors, and nail trimmers. Rabbits need to be brushed at least once a week to remove loose hair and get rid of any tangles and mats.

Most Angoras molt, or drop, their coat every two or three months. Some owners harvest Angora fur by clipping or plucking it.

wire brush

Fuzzy Features

When Angoras swallow too much of their hair, they can get a sickness called wool block. Grooming helps prevent wool block.

Angora fur harvesters must be very gentle when grooming and harvesting a rabbit's fur.

Spinning and Weaving

English and French Angoras produce 10 to 16 ounces (0.28 to 0.45 kg) of wool per year. Giant Angoras produce double that amount.

Spinning is the process by which Angora wool is made into yarn. Angora wool is very soft and thin. Spinning twists together two or more pieces of hair, making it stronger and tighter. Many people spin their Angora wool using hand spinners.

Weaving is the process by which yarn is made into **fabric**. Angora wool is woven into supersoft sweaters, scarves, and blankets.

Fuzzy Features

Angora wool is seven times warmer than sheep's wool.

This woman is spinning wool right off her Angora rabbit!

21

Wonderful Wool

Angora wool is used to make some of the softest, lightest, warmest fabrics in the world. We have Angora rabbits to thank for these beautiful products!

Angora rabbits are quiet, fearful animals. People who keep these rabbits and harvest their wool must be very careful when handling them so as not to frighten or harm them. People can show Angoras that they're thankful for their wool by treating them with kindness and respect. A well-cared-for rabbit produces the best wool of all.

GLOSSARY

burrow: To dig a hole in the ground for shelter.

coarse: Rough or wiry.

domesticated: Bred and raised for use by people.

fabric: A cloth produced by weaving or knitting.

harvest: To gather something after it's grown.

layered: Having parts lying over or under each other.

litter: A group of baby animals born to a mother animal all at one time.

pregnant: When a female has a baby or babies growing inside her.

texture: The feel or appearance of something.

tufty: Growing in tufts, or small clusters of long hairs.

INDEX

WEBSITES

Due to the changing nature of Internet links, PowerKids Press has developed an online list of websites related to the subject of this book. This site is updated regularly. Please use this link to access the list: www.powerkidslinks.com/wandw/angora